FAMOUS ATHLETES

STEPHEN CURRY

by Mari Schuh

CAPSTONE PRESS
a capstone imprint

Pebble Plus is published by Capstone Press,
1710 Roe Crest Drive, North Mankato, Minnesota 56003
www.capstonepub.com

Library of Congress Cataloging-in-Publication Data
Stephen Curry / by Mari Schuh.
     pages cm. — (Pebble Plus. Famous Athletes)
  Includes webography.
  Includes bibliographical references and index.
  Summary: "Presents the life of professional basketball athlete Stephen Curry in an
introductory biography with a timeline and photos"— Provided by publisher.
ISBN 978-1-4914-8509-5 (library binding)
ISBN 978-1-4914-8529-3 (paperback)
ISBN 978-1-4914-8525-5 (eBook PDF)
1. Curry, Stephen, 1988-—Juvenile literature. 2. Basketball players—United
States—Biography—Juvenile literature. I. Title.
  GV884.C88S38 2016
  796.323092—dc23
  [B]   2015021136

Note to Parents and Teachers

The Famous Athletes supports national curriculum standards for
social studies related to people, places, and culture. This book
describes and illustrates Stephen Curry. The images support
early readers in understanding the text. The repetition of words
and phrases helps early readers learn new words. This book also
introduces early readers to subject-specific vocabulary words,
which are defined in the Glossary section. Early readers may need
assistance to read some words and to use the Table of Contents,
Glossary, Read More, Internet Sites, and Index sections of the book.

Printed and bound in the United States.
042016 009710R

TABLE OF CONTENTS

1988

born in
Akron, Ohio

EARLY LIFE

Basketball star Stephen Curry was born March 14, 1988. He grew up watching and playing basketball. His dad played in the NBA. Stephen watched his dad's games.

NBA stands for National Basketball Association.

Stephen (right) talks with his brother, Seth (left), after his brother's game.

1988

born in
Akron, Ohio

Stephen grew up in Charlotte, North Carolina. He played basketball with his brother Seth. They played in their backyard. They played for hours.

1988
born in
Akron, Ohio

**2005
2006**
earns all-
conference and
all-state honors as
a junior
and senior

Stephen was a star player in high school. He led the basketball team to three conference titles. The team also played in the state playoffs. Stephen earned all-conference and all-state honors in 2005 and 2006.

1988
born in
Akron, Ohio

**2005
2006**
earns all-
conference and
all-state honors as
a junior
and senior

2008
leads Davidson
Wildcats to
victories in the
NCAA
Tournament

COLLEGE YEARS

After high school Stephen went to Davidson College in North Carolina. In 2008 he led his team to victories in the NCAA Tournament. He was named to All-American teams in 2008 and 2009.

NCAA stands for National Collegiate Athletic Association.

1988	2005 2006	2008	2008– 2009
born in Akron, Ohio	earns all-conference and all-state honors as a junior and senior	leads Davidson Wildcats to victories in the NCAA Tournament	becomes top college scorer

Stephen was one of the best shooters in college basketball. He led the nation in scoring for the 2008-2009 season. He scored an average of 28.6 points a game.

1988 born in Akron, Ohio

2005 2006 earns all-conference and all-state honors as a junior and senior

2008 leads Davidson Wildcats to victories in the NCAA Tournament

2008– 2009 becomes top college scorer

NBA STAR

In 2009 Stephen started playing in the NBA. He played well his first season. Stephen scored an average of 17.5 points a game. He was runner-up for the Rookie of the Year Award.

2009
starts to play for the NBA's Golden State Warriors

1988	2005 2006	2008	2008– 2009
born in Akron, Ohio	earns all-conference and all-state honors as a junior and senior	leads Davidson Wildcats to victories in the NCAA Tournament	becomes top college scorer

Stephen earned more awards.

In 2011 he won the

NBA Sportsmanship Award.

It is given to a player who plays

fair and respects others.

starts to play for
the NBA's
Golden State
Warriors

wins NBA
Sportsmanship
Award

1988 born in Akron, Ohio

2005 2006 earns all-conference and all-state honors as a junior and senior

2008 leads Davidson Wildcats to victories in the NCAA Tournament

2008– 2009 becomes top college scorer

Stephen is one of the NBA's best shooters. He led the NBA in three-point goals for three seasons in a row. He has also played in the All-Star Game two times.

starts to play for the NBA's Golden State Warriors

wins NBA Sportsmanship Award

Stephen (front, second from right) celebrates the NBA championship with his team.

1988
born in Akron, Ohio

2005 2006
earns all-conference and all-state honors as a junior and senior

2008
leads Davidson Wildcats to victories in the NCAA Tournament

2008–2009
becomes top college scorer

Stephen was named Most Valuable Player for the 2014-2015 season. He also helped his team win the NBA championship in 2015. Stephen wants to win many more games.

2009
starts to play for the NBA's Golden State Warriors

2011
wins NBA Sportsmanship Award

2015
named MVP for the 2014-2015 season

GLOSSARY

All-Star Game—a special game played every year in which the best NBA players play against each other

average—a number found by adding all scores together and dividing by the number of scores

championship—a contest or tournament that decides which team is the best

nference—a group of basketball teams from different universities that play against one another

NBA—National Basketball Association

NCAA—the National Collegiate Athletic Association, which runs college basketball

playoffs—a series of games played after the regular season to decide a championship

respect—to treat others in a polite and honest way

rookie—a player who is playing his or her first year on a team

runner-up—a player that takes second place

season—a time of the year; the NBA's regular season starts in the fall and ends in the spring.

title—an award given to the winner of a tournament

CRITICAL THINKING
USING THE COMMON CORE

1. How did Stephen's childhood help him become a basketball star? (Key Ideas and Details)

2. Stephen won the NBA Sportsmanship Award in 2011. How did he behave to get this award? Why is this award important? (Integration of Knowledge and Ideas)

READ MORE

Doeden, Matt. *All About Basketball*. North Mankato, Minn.: Capstone Press, 2015.

Lindeen, Mary. *Let's Play Basketball!* Chicago: Norwood House Press, 2015.

Nagelhout, Ryan. *I Love Basketball*. New York: Gareth Stevens Publishing, 2015.

Nelson, Robin. *Basketball is Fun*! Minneapolis, Minn.: Lerner Publications, 2014.

INTERNET SITES

FactHound offers a safe, fun way to find Internet sites related to this book. All of the sites on FactHound have been researched by our staff.

Here's all you do:

Visit *www.facthound.com*

Type in this code: 9781491485095

Check out projects, games and lots more at
www.capstonekids.com

23

INDEX

Editorial Credits
Gina Kammer, editor; Juliette Peters, designer;
Eric Gohl, media researcher; Lori Barbeau, production specialist

Photo Credits
Getty Images: NBAE/Andrew D. Bernstein, 4, NBAE/Don Smith, 14, NBAE/Tim
Cattera, 6; Lila J & Arnold W Photography: 8; Newscom: Cal Sport Media/Albert
Pena, cover, Cal Sport Media/John Green, 1, 16, EPA/Larry W. Smith, 20, Icon
SMI/David Allio, 12, MCT/David T. Foster III, 10, USA Today Sports/Derick E.
Hingle, 18

Design Elements: Shutterstock